Nothing's the End of the World

Poems by **Sara Holbrook**

Drawings by **J. J. Smith-Moore**

Wordsong/Boyds Mills Press

To my partners-in-rhyme, Katie and Kelly
— S. H.

To my sister Deborah
— J. J. S.-M.

Text copyright © 1995 by Sara Holbrook
Illustrations copyright © 1995 by Boyds Mills Press
All rights reserved

Published by Wordsong
Boyds Mills Press, Inc.
A Highlights Company
815 Church Street
Honesdale, Pennsylvania 18431
Printed in China

U.S. Cataloging-in-Publication Data
(Library of Congress Standards)

Holbrook, Sara.
    Nothing's the end of the world / poems by Sara Holbrook ;
drawings by J. J. Smith-Moore.—1st pbk. ed.
[48]p. : ill. ;   cm.
Summary : Original poems about the emotional upheavals of young love,
bothersome siblings, savvy substitute teachers, and more.
ISBN 1-56397-198-4 (pbk.)
1. Conduct of life—Poetry. 2. American poetry.
I. Smith-Moore, J. J., 1955-. II. Title.
811.54 21 2001 CIP AC
93-061164

First edition, 1995
First Wordsong paperback edition, 2001
Book designed by Tim Gillner
The text of this book is set in 14-point Garamond.
The illustrations are done in pen and ink.

10 9 8 7 6 5 4 3 2

CONTENTS

NOTHING'S THE END OF THE WORLD

Mother Nature is my mentor.
She tells me I'll be back,
even when my brain gets bruised
and my heart takes forty whacks.

That when I kick up storms
and my wind and hail bring pain,
she shows me sun can shine
after hostile hurricanes.

That breathless, cliff-clinging highs
and pelican-plunging lows
crest and fall like waves,
and I can surf in this natural flow.

That every stage
seems reasonable,
if I look at life
as seasonal.

That what slips and goes deep
finally rises.
That what's dull
hoptoads with surprises.

That even strip-mine wounds
can heal,
and the promise of spring
is real.

That sand in an oyster
may pearl,
and that NOTHING'S
the end of the world.

VICTIMIZED

I'm the victim
of the worst haircut
that ever sat on a head.
It took twenty minutes
and fifteen bucks.
I wanted a TRIM,
instead,
I got weedwhacked
in a shear attack
by that scissor-handed fiend.
My friends will laugh
and hoot and gasp.
I'm a fall-down,
fright-wig scream.

Life can be so mean.

BAD JOKE

Glasses and braces?
Is this some bad joke?
A conspiracy
so I look like a dope?
Plastic bug eyes
and tinsel buckteeth.
What'd I do to
deserve this grief?

Why can't I feel normal?
Why can't I feel good?
I'm hopeless and helpless
and misunderstood.
I can't stand this age,
and it's just my luck . . .
I'll turn out to be bald
when I finally grow up.

I HAVE TO STAND BY SUSAN TODD?

I have to stand by Susan Todd?
That's the worst.
Not me.
I'd rather face
a firing squad.
Who said
it must be
short to tall
at concerts;
alphabetical
would be more fair.
But please,
not me.
Not there.
Susan Todd can't
sing on key.
She sings so bad
my neck hairs jump.
Her voice creates
eardrum goose bumps.

It squints my eyes,
it curls my toes.
I know she tries
to find the notes,
but her screeching search
is like the scrape
of blackboards
by a metal rake.

Just this once?
Give me a break.

PAIRS

Parents are like mittens,
supposed to come in pairs,
and when they come in singles
it really isn't fair.

Would you be satisfied
with buying single socks?
Or settle for one hand
mounted on a clock?

Can't life be more like shopping,
where all the shoes have mates?
Where you can pick out what you want,
and return stuff if it breaks?

IT'S TODAY?

Frantic
panic,
sinking
sorrow.

The science test
is not
tomorrow.

MISERY

If misery loves company,
then I could use a crowd—
a stadium of miserables
crying with me . . . Loud!

Ten thousand people blubbering,
their twenty thousand eyes
swelled in tearful sympathy,
a woeful, wailing symphony,
audible a mile.
Then . . . maybe . . .
I would smile.

GROWN-UPS

I can't do
until they let me.
If I do,
that's when they get me.

I have to ask.
They get to tell.
I must keep still.
They get to yell.

Sometimes they say yes,
and then they refuse.
Then I get to plead,
and they get to choose.
And sometimes I win.
And sometimes I lose.

I WANT TO MOVE ACROSS THE STREET

I want to move
across the street
where the crackers aren't stale
and the closets are neat.

Where the furniture's polished,
and the carpets are swept,
and the scissors are found
where the scissors are kept.

Where they're not out of milk,
and no one is late,
you can always find house keys,
both sneakers, and tape.

Where nobody swears,
hogs the last slice of bread,
fights over chairs
or wishes me dead.

Across the street
the fruit's never brown,
and nobody's yelling to
"Turn that thing down!"

I want to move to a new home
where the loudest sound
is the telephone.
To where Mrs. Wilson lives . . .
alone.

DO YOU EVER LISTEN?

Do you ever listen?
Do you ever hear?
Not even if I took a trumpet
and blew it in your ear.

Well, maybe I'm too busy
for listening to you.
Maybe I won't hear
when you tell me what to do.

COUNTDOWN TO GET UP

Beneath
a hug of covers,
snugglebuggled
in my bed,
I count down—
ready—set—
I'm gonna get up. . . .
Instead,
I beg for two more minutes
from my heartless,
ticking clock.
I'm about as energetic
as a ten-ton-moss-grown rock.

As I pass
my last
drop-deadline,
I snugglebuggle deeper.
Must we all be up for learning?
I'm already a summa cum laude sleeper.

GOOD EARS

My teacher has good ears.
She proves it all the time.
If eight kids fake a sneeze,
she knows which sneeze is mine.

Her back turned toward the class,
and writing on the board,
she can even hear the silent drop
of spitballs on the floor.

And doesn't have to turn around,
or even look at all
before she says,
"Okay, my friend,
you may stand in the hall."

I think she has to have
microphones somewhere;
she's picking up on signals
from antennas in her hair.

SNOW NEWS IS GOOD NEWS

What if Nature
slipped up?
We all make mistakes,
and snow news
is good news.
Why study?
Let's play.
The test could be cancelled,
don't book this great day
away.

It's not beyond hoping . . .
a snow day
in May.

SUMMER

Celebrate.
Jump and shout.
Summer's in.
School is out.

OUT OF CONTROL

The cake was for the company;
I went out of control.
I just couldn't stop
once I licked the bowl.

I'm dead meat,
that's for sure.
While she was getting dressed,
I couldn't help myself.
I slivered it to death.

WHO ME?

I never pass out gossip.
I never peek through doors.
I've never copied homework.
I've never muddied floors.
I never stole a candy,
especially not before a meal.
I wouldn't spoil my appetite.
Besides,
I never steal.

I never disappoint
or tell a secret
or make another person cry.
I'm practically a saint.
You can trust me.
Would I lie?

SUBSTITUTE

Substitute.
Substitute.
Let's trade seats;
pretend you're mute.
Say Jamie's in a coma,
and our teacher
gives no homework.
Say Frankie's deaf
and Cindy's blind.
Hide that chair.
You—over here.
You—over there.
She'll never find
who made her stand.

Rats.
She has a seating plan.

QUICK REACTION

It's simply my reaction.
Who cares
what it's about.
I reach for satisfaction
with my tongue.
I stick it out.

It's more secret than
a scream,
and quicker than
a pout.
When it hurts to hold it in,
I just smile
and stick it out.

NOT FORGOT

I forgot to take the trash out;
    you didn't tell me that's my job.
I forgot to bring my money;
    you never know when you'll get robbed.
I forgot that game at six;
    I needed a little quiet.
I forgot to feed the dog,
    but then, she really needs a diet.
I forgot to wear my gloves;
    of course, I inherited hot hands.
I forgot to do my project,
    but I described such detailed plans.

You're right,
I forgot today was Tuesday.
    That storm must have stopped the clock.
But don't think I'm absentminded,
    with the brains of a preschool block,
I'm teaching myself to be creative
    by making up what I forgot.

MAY I BE EXCUSED?

At dinner she said,
"Nice cat, is he yours?"

"Yeah, he is," I said.
"He hardly gets fur balls at all.
When he does?
He goes right outside to spit.
And he eats all his food
'fore the maggots get it,
most times."

I said, "Pass the rice.

"Once a dead squirrel
was behind the garage—
no one's fault, natural causes.
It was twelve times its size
'cause it swelled from the heat?
Kids came and saw it
(ten cents a peek),
but the maggots got it
after a week or so, really sick."

I said, "Pass the meat.

"One summer
the trash cans got maggots
so bad I thought I would vomit.
So I called my dad,
who cleaned them himself
with a poison
he keeps on the shelf.
He said if I touched it
my fingers would melt."

I said, "Pass the milk.

"I once touched a bird and got lice."

She put down her fork
and just said,
"How nice."

LOCAL UNION NEEDED

Clean the cat box?
Do the dishes?
Make the bed?

YOU
feed the fish!
'Cause as of now
I'm on strike.
Give me a raise
or I'll take a hike.

I gotta find a union.
Where's my brother, anyway?
No one else around here works.
I want equal rest and better pay.

Okay.
I'll take the trash out.
Okay.
I act like a pain.
But after all, at my age,
it's ALSO my job to complain.

INVASION

Same as always,
I came in at four,
up those back stairs
and through that old door.
Only to find the place
had been raided
by unwelcome swells
of smells I just hated.
An army of cans,
their tin hats undone,
peppers and spoons,
a naked onion.
While I was at school,
you think it was nice?
Invading my kitchen
with yuck—Spanish rice?

HOPELESS

My dad is so stupid.
My dad is so dumb.
He calls the wrong name
when he wants me to come.

He calls me
Barbara-Bob-Stacey,
and I answer,
"Who?"
Then he slaps at his forehead
and yells,
"Number 2!"

"You're hopeless,"
I tell him,
and then he gets riled.
But what gives
when a man
doesn't know
his own child?

LEAVES

Sure,
I like to jump in leaves.
I also like to sit.
There's raking to be done?
Don't trick me into it
with promises of fun.
It sounds like work.
No way.
Just call me for the part
when it is time to play.

MY BROTHER

My brother is
    a redwood,
wedged between my toes.

My brother is
    a basketball,
jammed up in my nose.

My brother is
    a scratchy coat,
cut too small to fit.

My brother's
    a mosquito,
just begging to get hit.

My brother is
    a chain saw,
that once started whines and roars.

My brother is
    the chicken pox.
He cannot be ignored.

ANGRY

I'm angry.
Foot stomping,
door kicking,
wall hitting,
book throwing,
desk slapping,
drawer slamming,
pencil breaking,
teacher hating,
paper tearing,
teeth baring
mad.

The worst part is,
can't you see?
There's no one else to blame
but me.

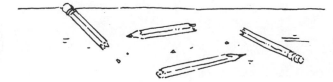

WAITING

Is there a better name
for gloom
than
the Vice-Principal's waiting room?

Is there a deeper,
darker well
than
Mr. Hansen's holding cell?

A snowball in a microwave
has a better life expectancy
than me stuck in this fiery grave
with everyone's eyes dissecting me.

One on one with Hansen's bad enough,
but first, I have to sweat this lobby.
Detention's nothing but a deadweight drag.
I gotta find a better hobby.

TO COVER A SPOT

I dropped a lie
to cover a spot . . .
but the lie didn't fit
e x a c t l y,
and it grew a lot,
         that spot.
So I sprinkled some more
to cover the mess,
the spreading spot,
so no one would guess
         I lied.
But the spot grew deep
and oceanwide.
It soaked up every
cover I tried,
         that spot.
When it first appeared,
it was quiet and small,
the cover-up lies
didn't help at all,
         in fact,
one spot, one drop, grew
into a million gallons of mess,
and now I will have so much
more to confess.

I WISH I HADN'T SAID IT

I wish I hadn't said it.
I wish I never breathed.
That question was so stupid,
I could crawl up my sleeve.

Everyone was looking.
I thought I saw a smirk.
The whole class saw me blushing
and thinks that I'm a jerk.

I'm going to sew my mouth shut.
Or jump,
which way's the ledge?
Embarrassment like that
is worse,
by far,
than death.

HELP ME, PLEASE

Check the closet.
On your knees,
under the table,
help me, please,
in the toy box,
search the floor,
in the fridge,
behind that door,
on the bookshelf,
on the stairs,
quick, the toilet,
move those chairs,
in the dryer,
behind that picture,
check the drawer,
the light fixture,
of course I'm sure,
and I'm scared plenty.
I looked there twice.
The cage is empty.

LEAVE-BEHINDS

Edison thought up the light bulb,
records and phonographs.
Curie perfected the X-ray;
Knute Rockne, the forward pass.

Salk made vaccinations;
Ford, the Model T;
Disney, Mickey Mouse,
and I—
watch my TV.

I'm nestled in this world
that bold inventors built.
Will my leave-behinds
be just my junk food trash
and guilt?

What made two bicycle makers fly?
What made my couch potato state?
What if I turned off the tube
and let my leisure time create?

I wonder what I'd make.

LEADER OF THE PACK

I dream I am so cool,
a leader of the pack,
friends anywhere I choose
in a finger snap.

In dreams I sparkle
as I win.
I tell jokes
and others grin.

And everybody copies me
and how I dress and talk.
I am followed by my wannabes
every time I walk
from lunch or gym.
I am famous, but still nice.
I am thoughtful and polite.

I know there's pressure
when you're cooler than the rest,
but I can take the stress.
In dreams I'm never warm and flat
like pop left capless in the sun.
That's why dreams are fun.

CALLED ON

He called on me.
My answer's wrong.
Caught like a squirrel
on an open lawn.

Standing alone,
twiddling my paws,
frozen in place,
working my jaws.

I'd like to bolt,
but where?
I moan.
Could anyone
be more
alone?

TRYOUTS

If I try out,
what's the worst?
The worst is
I might lose,
not be the one they choose.

I could say it didn't matter;
I was kidding when I tried.
Then everyone would know
I lost and then I lied.

Or I could shrug and say,
"So what, I lost,
I'm only a beginner."
Besides,
if I never try,
I'll never be a winner.

MY DREAMS

Open
window by my bed,
the EXIT
for my dreams.
Among the light-lured bugs,
mobbed against the screen,
my dreams
step out at night,
stretch,
and vanish
out of sight.

SOMEDAY

Brothers and sisters,
like heat rash and blisters,
get me twitchin' till I start to burn.

It's a natural reaction,
that gets worse when I'm scratchin'.
Someday,
they all say,
I will learn.
And this awful annoyance
will become an enjoyance,
that THE PAIN will no longer be hot.

That the itching will end,
that we'll grow up best friends.
Emphatically,
I answer,
"Not."

WHY DO THEY CALL THAT LOVE?

Here's what I don't understand.
If Tracy gets limp
when she looks at Jack,
but when Tracy walks by,
Jack turns his back.

Why do they call that love?

If Jack's loving Liz and
Lizzie loves Paul, but
Paul says Liz is much too tall,
so Paul wants Sue who
stays true blue
to some guy who moved away.
So she writes and cries all day.

Why do they call that love?

I know Natalie loves the hardest,
but forever never lasts long.
And Bobby doesn't love anyone
till after she has gone.
And they even call that love.

Is love some game of tee ball?
We all take turns at the plate?
No one knows how to catch,
the score's 40-38?

Love has to get it together or
it's only make-believe.
What's the use in hitting
if there's no one to receive?

Love, it's a game with no innings,
no rules or end of the season.
Tell me, then, what is the reason
this game has so many fans.

That's what I don't understand.

MY WAY IS BETTER

Your way's
okay,
I guess you could say.
Okay.
But my way is better.

I won't whine or complain,
and you won't get blamed
when we fail,
'cause my way is better.

I'm too old to say "NO!"
in a loud stomping show.
Of course a small "told you so"
might escape from me though,
so okay.

But my way is better.

CONVERSATION

I'd like it
if you called
just to ask me what I think,
not to tell me you're depressed
because the Oilers stink.

I'd like it
if you asked, just once,
"How'd that movie make you feel?"
instead of telling me to chill
because the violence
wasn't real.

I'd like it
if you questioned more
and put your expertise on hold.
I'd like
a conversation
and I'm tired of
getting told.

THIS CAN'T BE

I'm in love with Adelle,
with her swishy-swish walk,
with her breeze-by-me smells,
and her giggle-girl talk.

Don't tell.
This can't be!
Am I weak in the head?
She smiles.
I can't breathe,
and a stop sign's less red
than my face.

This can't be!

Heart and feet start to race
and I stumble.
She says,
"Did you have a nice trip?"
Oh, please,
quiver-knees, would you
just get a grip?
Let me walk like I'm cool,
get me out of this school.

I'm betrayed.
This can't be!
But my blabbermouth body
is telling on me.